P9-CSA-056

The IMPORTANT THING About MARGARET WISE BROWN

Written by
Mac Barnett

Illustrated by
Sarah Jacoby

BALZER + BRAY
An Imprint of HarperCollinsPublishers

The author and illustrator gratefully acknowledge the help of
Lindsey Wyckoff, Jim Boone, Jim Rockefeller, Leonard Marcus, Thacher Hurd,
the Vinalhaven Land Trust, Beth S. Harris, Allie Jane Bruce,
Jennifer Brown, Cynthia Weill, and Elizabeth Bird.

SOURCES

BOOKS

Brown, Margaret Wise. "Creative Writing for Very Young Children." *The Book of Knowledge Annual 1951*. Edited by E. V. McLoughlin. New York: Grolier Society, 1951.

Brown, Margaret Wise. "Stories to Be Sung and Songs to Be Told." *The Book of Knowledge Annual 1952*. Edited by E. V. McLoughlin. New York: Grolier Society, 1952.

Gary, Amy. *In the Great Green Room: The Brilliant and Bold Life of Margaret Wise Brown*. New York: Flatiron Books, 2017.

Greene, Carol. *Margaret Wise Brown: Author of Goodnight Moon*. Chicago: Children's Press, 1993.

Lepore, Jill. *The Mansion of Happiness: A History of Life and Death*. New York: Alfred A. Knopf, 2012.

Marcus, Leonard, ed. *Dear Genius: The Letters of Ursula Nordstrom*. New York: HarperCollins, 1998.

Marcus, Leonard. *Margaret Wise Brown: Awakened by the Moon*. Boston: Beacon Press, 1992.

Mitchell, Lucy Sprague. *Here and Now Story Book*. New York: E. P. Dutton & Company, 1921.

Moore, Anne Carol. *Nicholas: A Manhattan Christmas Story*. New York: G. P. Putnam and Sons, 1924.

And of course: the many stories, poems, and songs of Margaret Wise Brown.

ARTICLES

Brown, Margaret Wise. "Writing for Children." *Hollins* alumnae magazine. Winter, 1949.

Pichey, Martha. "Bunny Dearest." *Vanity Fair*, December 2000, 172–183.

Rockefeller, James. "Margaret Wise Brown: Writer of Songs and Nonsense." *Island Journal* (Vinalhaven, ME), 1994, 46–50.

COLLECTIONS

Brown, Margaret Wise. Papers, 1938–1960. Hollins University Special Collections.

Brown, Margaret Wise. "Writing for Five Year Olds." Research paper, Bank Street School of Education, 1939.

Moore, Anne Carol. Papers, 1898–1960. New York Public Library Humanities and Sciences Library Manuscripts and Archives Division. NYPL Digital Collections.

Vinalhaven Historical Society.

Balzer + Bray is an imprint of HarperCollins Publishers. The Important Thing About Margaret Wise Brown. Text copyright © 2019 by Mac Barnett. Illustrations copyright © 2019 by Sarah Jacoby. All rights reserved. Manufactured in China. No part of this book may be used or reproduced in any manner whatsoever without written permission except in the case of brief quotations embodied in critical articles and reviews. For information address HarperCollins Children's Books, a division of HarperCollins Publishers, 195 Broadway, New York, NY 10007. www.harpercollinschildrens.com. Library of Congress Control Number: 2018943094. ISBN 978-0-06-239344-9. The artist used watercolor, Nupastel, and Photoshop magic to create the illustrations for this book. Typography by Dana Fritts.

19 20 21 22 23 SCP 10 9 8 7 6 5 4 3 2 1 ❖ First Edition

To the people at Bank Street,
here and now,
there and then.

—M.B.

To Mom and Katie, you are very important.

—S.J.

"It did not seem important that
any one wrote these stories. They were true.
And it still doesn't seem important!
All this emphasis today on who writes what
seems silly to me as far as
children are concerned."

—Margaret Wise Brown

Margaret Wise Brown lived for 42 years.
This book is 42 pages long.
You can't fit somebody's life into 42 pages,
so I am just going to tell you some important things.

1

The important thing about Margaret Wise Brown is that she wrote books.
Every book was written by somebody.
Some books were written by Ruth Krauss.
Some books were written by Jon Scieszka or Judith Viorst.
The book you are reading now was written by Mac Barnett.
Over 100 books were written by Margaret Wise Brown.

3

It can be odd to imagine the lives of the people who write the books you read,
like running into your teacher at the supermarket.
But authors are people.
They are born and they die.
They make jokes and mistakes.
They fall in love and they fall in love again.
They go to the supermarket to buy tomatoes,
which they keep in the bottom drawers of their refrigerators,
even though tomatoes should stay out on the counter.
But which of these things is important? And to whom?

What is important about Margaret Wise Brown?
Well, what do you want to know?
When is her birthday?
May 23, 1910.
What color was her hair?
Golden, the color of timothy hay.
Did she ever fall in love?
Yes, with a woman called Michael
and a man called Pebble.
Did she have a dog?
She had lots.
What was her favorite dog's name?
His name was Crispin's Crispian.
Was he a good boy?
She thought so, but he bit lots of people.
Is any of this important?
Why do you ask?
What is important about Margaret Wise Brown?

When Margaret Wise Brown was six

or seven
and she lived in a house next to the woods,
she kept many pets.
A dog and
two squirrels.
Seven fish,
a pair of guinea pigs,
a wild robin,
and thirty-six rabbits.

This is a story about a rabbit.
Margaret's rabbits lived in a great big hutch.
At first there were a few,
and then there were many.
That's how it is with rabbits.
They are born,
and they die,

and when one of Margaret's rabbits died,
she skinned that rabbit
and wore its pelt.
Margaret wrapped herself in that rabbit's fur
and paraded before her brother and sisters
(and the other rabbits as well).

There are people who will say a story like this
doesn't belong in a children's book.
But it happened.
Margaret Wise Brown took up a rabbit
and took off its pelt,
and she did it when she was a child.
And isn't it important that children's books
contain the things children think of
and the things children do,
even if those things seem strange?

This is a story about a rabbit.
The rabbit must go to bed,
and he takes a long time
saying goodnight to everything.
Nobody knows why he says goodnight
to all this stuff—
his socks and some mush and even the a
but I have an idea.
I think it is because he is afraid to go to
Have you read this book?
Do you know what I mean?

This is a story about a rabbit.
He is trying to escape from his mother.
But his mother just won't let him get away.
(Maybe that is why he is trying
to escape from her.)

This is not a story about a rabbit.

But when this book was first published, do you know
what its cover was made of?

The cover of this book was made from the fur of a rabbit.

Every copy was wrapped up in a real rabbit's fur.

What do you think of that?

People thought Margaret Wise Brown was strange,
and they thought her books were strange too.

Now it's true that Margaret Wise Brown did strange things.

She swam naked in cold water.

She put a door in her house that led out to a cliff that plunged into the sea.

And when Margaret Wise Brown first got paid to write a book,

do you know what she did with the money?

Margaret Wise Brown found a flower cart
on a street in the city
and she bought the whole thing.
Not the cart.
Not the horse.
But every last flower.

Margaret Wise Brown filled her little home
with flowers
and she threw a party and invited her friends.

After a few hours her friends left.
And after a few days the flowers died.
Some people might think it's silly
or sad
to spend so much money
on something that is over so soon.
But I think it is beautiful.
How about you?

Now it's true that Margaret Wise Brown wrote strange books.
In her books, you would turn the page
and the story would suddenly change.
Sometimes a duck would appear for no reason.
And the narrator would often stop telling the story
and ask the reader a question.
Now isn't that a strange thing to do?

Some people,
when they see something strange,
become bothered.
These people build worlds that make perfect sense,
even if that means ignoring many strange things
around them.

Now here is something I believe.
(I know there are only 23 pages left in this book,
but it's important.)
No good book is loved by everyone,
and any good book is bound to bother somebody.
Because every good book is at least a little bit strange,
and there are some people who do not
like strange things in their worlds.

Anne Carroll Moore was a librarian,
and her world was a room in the New York Public Library.
It was a world she built,
with plants and candles
and small tables and chairs
and shelves full of books for children.

The New York Public Library
is guarded by two stone lions
on the steps out front.
And the Children's Room
was guarded by Anne Carroll Moore.

Anne Carroll Moore was a conservative.
She liked books that were darling and innocent,
like she thought children should be.
When Anne Carroll Moore read
the right kind of book,
it got its own place on
a little shelf
in the library.

And when Anne Carroll Moore read
the wrong kind of book,
she picked up a big rubber stamp,
which she slammed down
BAM!
and which said:
NOT RECOMMENDED FOR
PURCHASE BY EXPERT

And the book did not get a place
on a shelf in that library,
nor in many other libraries besides,
because lots of librarians listened to
Anne Carroll Moore.
She was important.

So Anne Carroll Moore would sit at her desk
with a stack of books
and a rubber stamp
and a wooden doll named Nicholas Knickerbocker.

Nicholas Knickerbocker went everywhere with Ms. Moore.
He had his own luggage.
And he had his own bed.

And if you ever had dinner at Anne Carroll Moore's house,
you might find yourself sitting next to Nicholas Knickerbocker,
who had his own plate and a fork and a knife.
And you'd have to ask him, "How do you do?"

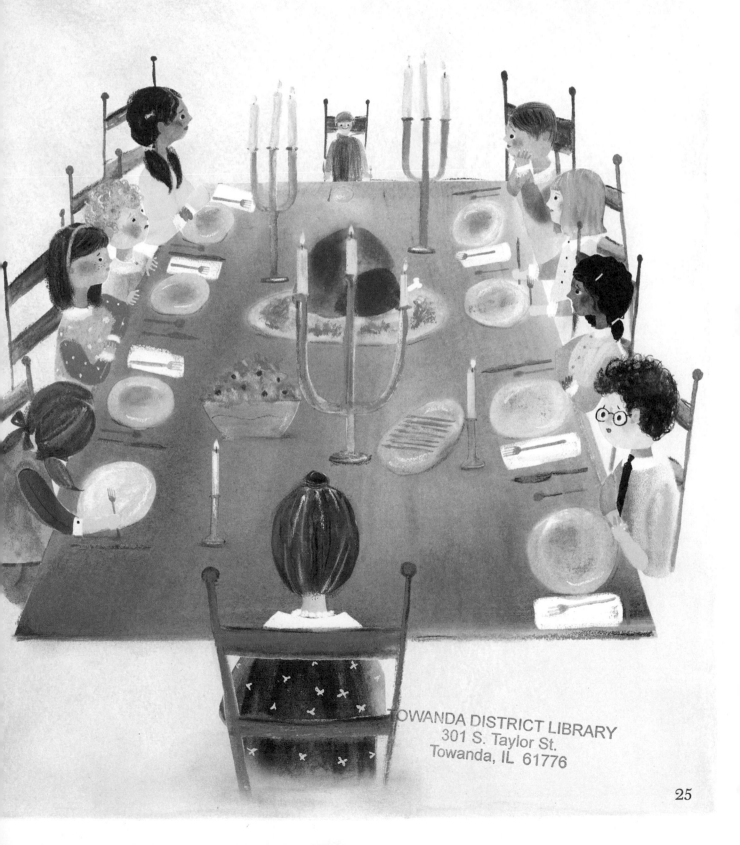

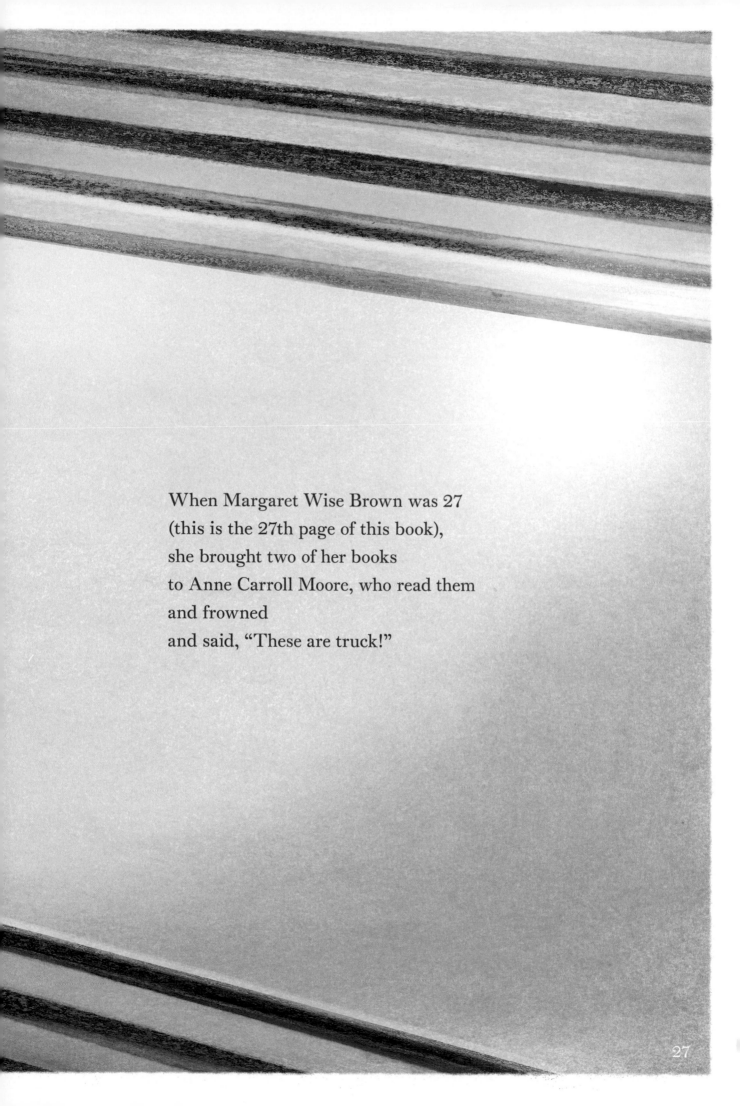

When Margaret Wise Brown was 27
(this is the 27th page of this book),
she brought two of her books
to Anne Carroll Moore, who read them
and frowned
and said, "These are truck!"

"Truck" is not good.
"Truck" means worthless;
it means garbage.
Anne Carroll Moore thought
these were the wrong kind of books.

But do you know what Nicholas Knickerbocker thought?

Nothing.
Nicholas Knickerbocker was
made of wood.
He didn't have a brain.

Margaret Wise Brown's books
NOT RECOMMENDED FOR
PURCHASE BY EXPERT.

And so this book
did not get to come into the library.

And this book
did not get to come into the library.

And even this book
(which you've probably read,
and if you haven't,
you should)
did not get to come into the library.

By the time *Goodnight Moon* was written,
Anne Carroll Moore had retired,
but she'd still go to her old desk,
which was now someone else's,
someone named Frances,
and she'd tear up the list
of books Frances liked
and put down a list of her own.
(Though to be fair, I don't think Frances
liked *Goodnight Moon* either.)

In fact, there was a time when
even Margaret Wise Brown
did not get to come into the library.
I know we are nearing the end of this book,
which has only 42 pages, but this is
important.

There was once a tea party
at the New York Public Library.
Authors were there,
and illustrators were there,
and Anne Carroll Moore was there,
and so was Frances.

But when Margaret Wise Brown
walked up the steps
to the front door,
she wasn't allowed inside.
(She didn't have an invitation.)

So, when people with invitations
walked up to the library,
do you know what they found,
right in the middle of the stairs?

35

They found two women,
Margaret Wise Brown
and her editor
(whose name was Ursula Nordstrom),
sitting there,
right in the middle of the stairs,
between the two lions
(whose names are Patience and Fortitude),
having a tea party of their own.

Margaret Wise Brown sat there drinking her tea
(I don't know for sure Margaret Wise Brown
wore a rabbit fur coat that day,
but we had to put her in something),
and if you wanted to get into the library,
you had to go around her.

We are getting close to page 42, which is
the last page of this book.
When Margaret Wise Brown turns 42,
she will take up her furs and her dog
(Crispin's Crispian, who bites)
and take off on a ship, across the ocean.

This was her plan: to get married to
somebody she loved very much
and to sail around the world.

But when Margaret Wise Brown is 42,
she will die in a hospital in France.

Lives don't work the way most books do.
They can end suddenly,
as fast as you kick your leg in the air.
Lives are funny and sad,
scary and comforting,
beautiful and ugly,
but not when they're supposed to be,
and sometimes all at the same time.
There are patterns in a life,
and patterns in a story,
but in real lives and good stories
the patterns are hard to see,
because the truth is never made of straight lines.
Lives are strange.
And there are people who do not like strange stories,
especially in books for children.

But sometimes you find a book that feels as strange as life does.

These books feel true.

These books are important.

Margaret Wise Brown wrote books like this,

and she wrote them for children,

because she believed children deserve important books.

The important thing about Margaret Wise Brown is that she wrote books.